Organ Transplantation

Ann Fullick

Heinemann

A L I S

www.heinemann.co.uk/library
Visit our website to find out more information about **Heinemann Library** books.

To order:
☎ Phone 44 (0) 1865 888066
▤ Send a fax to 44 (0) 1865 314091
▢ Visit the Heinemann Bookshop at www.heinemann.co.uk/library to browse our catalogue and order online.

First published in Great Britain by Heinemann Library, Halley Court, Jordan Hill, Oxford OX2 8EJ, a division of Reed Educational and Professional Publishing Ltd. Heinemann is a registered trademark of Reed Educational and Professional Publishing Ltd.

OXFORD MELBOURNE AUCKLAND JOHANNESBURG BLANTYRE
GABORONE IBADAN PORTSMOUTH NH (USA) CHICAGO

Designed by Tinstar Design (www.tinstar.co.uk)
Illustrations by Art Construction
Originated by Ambassador Litho Ltd.
Printed and bound in Hong Kong/China

ISBN 0 431 14880 5   (hardback)   ISBN 0 431 14887 2   (paperback)
06 05 04 03 02   06 05 04 03
10 9 8 7 6 5 4 3 2   10 9 8 7 6 5 4 3 2 1

British Library Cataloguing in Publication Data
Fullick, Ann
    Organ transplantation. – (Science at the edge)
    1. Transplantation of organs, tissues, etc. – Juvenile literature
    2. Transplantation of organs, tissues, etc. – Moral and ethical aspects – Juvenile literature
    I.Title
    617.9'5

Acknowledgements
The Publisher would like to thank the following for permission to reproduce photographs: Corbis: pp19B, 26, 31, Mary Ann McDonald p49 inset, Richard T Nowitz p53, Joseph Sohm p34; Environmental Images: p50; Frank Spooner Pictures: p39; Medical Photography Portsmouth Hospitals NHS Trust: pp23, 27, 33; Popperfoto: pp15, 19T, 41; Science Photo Library: pp5, 8, 10, 12, 22, 29, 32, 55, Sheila Terry p15, Chris Priest p37; Amanda Sheehan: pp27, 43, 47; Still Pictures: Pierre Gleizes p4, Mike Schroder p21; Topham Picturepoint: pp49, 57; Wellcome Medical Trust: pp11, 52; WENN/TV-AM: p45.

Cover photograph reproduced with permission of Still Pictures.

Thanks for their invaluable input to Lucy and Amanda Sheehan and the Sheehan family, Anne Walters and other members of the Wessex Renal Transplant team at Portsmouth.

Every effort has been made to contact copyright holders of any material reproduced in this book. Any omissions will be rectified in subsequent printings if notice is given to the Publisher.

Disclaimer
All the Internet addresses (URLs) given in this book were valid at the time of going to press. However, due to the dynamic nature of the Internet, some addresses may have changed, or sites may have changed or ceased to exist since publication. While the author and Publisher regret any inconvenience this may cause readers, no responsibility for any such changes can be accepted by either the author or the Publisher.

Any words appearing in the text in bold, **like this**, are explained in the Glossary.

Contents

The organs of the body

The human body is a masterpiece of biology. It enables us to move around to get food, escape danger, get to school on time, play football, baseball, cricket... More than that, the human body uses the food that we eat and turns it into more body or even new human beings. The body can get rid of poisons that may be taken in or produced by the body itself. It can survive in an enormous range of conditions, use tools, write books – and all these things are possible because of the complex biology going on inside it.

All of the activities of the body are made possible by major organs (collections of cells and **tissues** that carry out a major function in the body) working together to produce a co-ordinated whole. Each organ carries out a very specific job within the body. These major organs include the heart, which pumps the blood around the body, the **kidneys**, which balance the water levels in the body and get rid of waste, the eyes, which enable us to see, and the liver, which cleans and purifies the blood. The organs work together to maintain steady conditions inside the body, regardless of how it is being used or where it is.

The average human being contains billions of cells, miles of tubing, square metres of skin, litres of fluid and pounds of muscle. Somehow all of this body-stuff has to be organized to work, and work properly, whatever demands are put on the body.

What if things go wrong?

Almost everyone takes their body completely for granted – until something goes wrong. And if anything does go wrong with any of a person's major organs, they are in deep trouble – in fact the failure of a major organ can mean death. However, in the last 50 years, there has been an enormous increase in the number of people who survive the total failure of one of their body organs, thanks to the development of transplant surgery or organ transplantation. This involves giving a very sick person the healthy organs they need from someone else, often someone who has died very suddenly. There are many thousands of people around the world who are only alive and well today because they have someone else's heart, kidney, liver, lungs or small intestine working away inside their body, carrying out the important job that their own organ was no longer able to do.

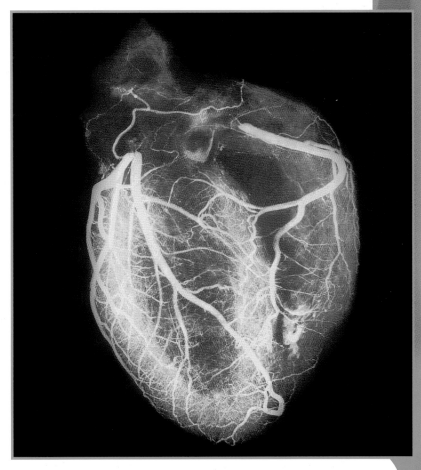

The idea that a complex organ like the heart can be removed and replaced with another one would have seemed completely unbelievable 100 years ago – yet now, every 27 minutes, someone somewhere in the world receives a transplanted organ!

How does the organization work?

The basic unit of a human being is a single cell – a jelly-like blob contained in a **membrane**. A cell carries out lots ands lots of chemical reactions at the same time. In large organisms, such as human beings, cells are often very specialized. This means they carry out one particular job. The structure of these cells is different from the 'basic model' in order to suit the very specialized jobs that they do.

The specialized cells are often grouped together to form a tissue. In human beings, connective tissue joins bits of the body together, while nervous tissue carries information around the body, and muscles move the body about.

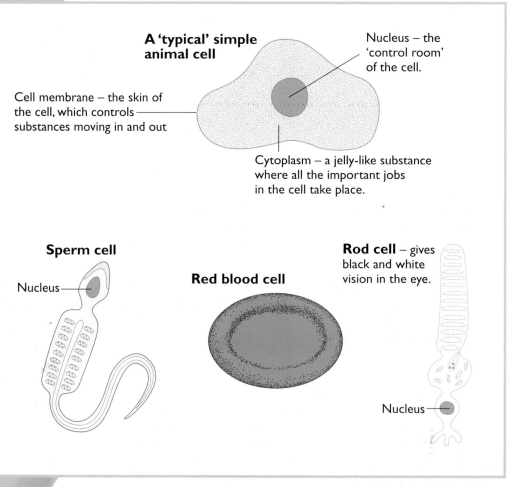

A 'typical' simple animal cell

Nucleus – the 'control room' of the cell.

Cell membrane – the skin of the cell, which controls substances moving in and out

Cytoplasm – a jelly-like substance where all the important jobs in the cell take place.

Sperm cell

Nucleus

Red blood cell

Rod cell – gives black and white vision in the eye.

Nucleus

Sometimes cells become so specialized that they only have one function within the body. Good examples of this include sperm, red blood cells and the specialized cells involved in colour vision in the human eye (rod cells).

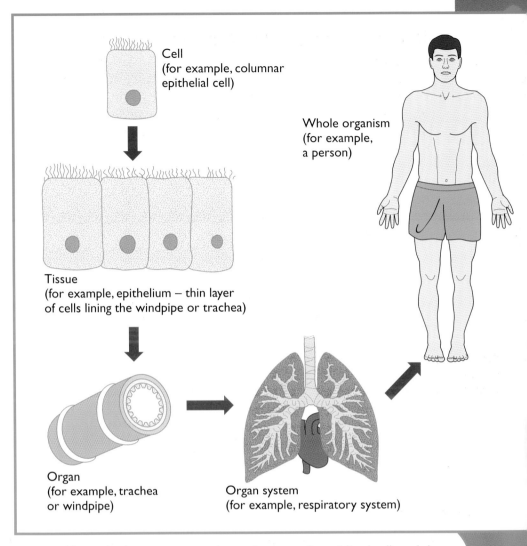

Cell
(for example, columnar
epithelial cell)

Whole organism
(for example,
a person)

Tissue
(for example, epithelium – thin layer
of cells lining the windpipe or trachea)

Organ
(for example, trachea
or windpipe)

Organ system
(for example, respiratory system)

Human body organs are made up of groups of specialized cells and the organ systems are designed to carry out very specific jobs – for example getting oxygen into the blood, pumping blood around the body or hearing what is going on in the environment.

In many living organisms, including human beings, there is another level of organization – several different tissues work together to form an organ such as the heart, the kidneys or the liver. Each of these organs has its own job. In turn, different organs are combined in **organ systems** to carry out major functions in the body, such as transporting the blood or reproduction.

A look at the work of some of the human organs and organ systems makes it all too clear why it is such a disaster if they go wrong.

The heart and lungs

The best-known human organs are the heart and the lungs. They are both vital for life, and they work together as a team, along with miles of tubing called blood vessels, to make up what is called the cardiovascular system. The heart is one of the earliest organs to be formed in the developing human **embryo**.

The heart is basically a bag of muscle that beats from a few weeks after a person is formed in the **uterus** until their death. It fills and empties, forcing blood out of the heart to where it is needed. The right-hand side of the heart sends blood to the lungs to pick up oxygen. The blood also gets rid of the poisonous **carbon dioxide** that has built up as a waste-product in the working cells of the body. The left-hand side of the heart sends oxygen-rich blood, which has been through the lungs, around the whole of the rest of the body, supplying all the cells with the oxygen they need for life.

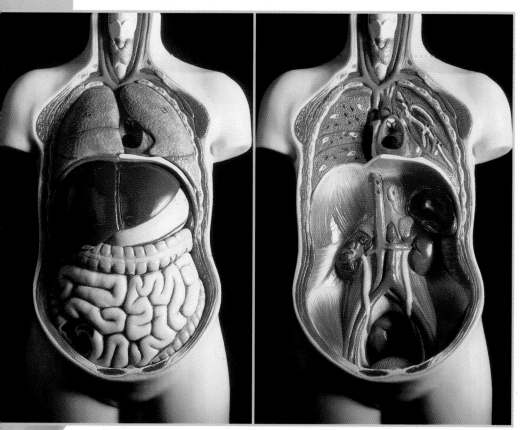

Inside everyone there are lots of different organs, all doing important jobs that help to keep us alive.

The heart is made up of muscle tissue that has its own rich blood supply. It also contains special tissue that makes up the valves of the heart – flaps that stop blood flowing in the wrong direction – and big blood vessels that allow blood to flow into and out of the heart.

The lungs take the blood from the body and pass it through specially adapted tiny **air sacs**. These make it possible for as much oxygen as possible to be picked up by the blood, and as much carbon dioxide as possible to be removed from the blood. The process is known as gaseous exchange, and it must take place efficiently if someone is to lead a healthy, active life.

A pair of kidneys

The kidneys remove **urea** from the system, a poisonous waste product that results from the breakdown of **protein** in the diet. They also remove excess salt and control the water balance of the body. This is enormously important – if the water balance goes wrong, all the cells in the body are in danger of either swelling or shrivelling up. Either way, they wouldn't work properly and death would not be far away!

Some organs, like lungs and kidneys, come in pairs – but why? Probably because these organs are so important they have a kind of 'built-in spare'. But if that is so, why do we only have one heart? No one is quite sure.

What does a liver do?

Most people know that they have a liver, but they are often unsure about where it is and what it does. The liver is one of the most important organs in the body – it carries out around 500 different jobs! It is involved in the control and management of the **carbohydrates**, proteins and fats we eat. It helps to remove and break down **cholesterol** and other fats and convert them into storage **molecules**. It breaks down excess proteins into urea – which can be excreted – and useful amino acids (the chemical building blocks of proteins). It stores a number of substances, makes bile (a liquid that helps in digestion), helps control the body temperature and breaks down some of the **toxins** taken into the body. And this happens on a regular basis, because substances such as alcohol and painkillers are toxins. In fact, the liver acts like a personal detoxification (poison-removal) plant, getting rid of harmful chemicals. So a liver is a very useful organ to have, and when the liver fails, the body is affected in a wide number of ways, several of which can lead to death.

Organ failure!

Most people are born with a set of perfectly healthy organs which then go on to work throughout their life. After 70, 80, 90 or even 100 years, their heart, **kidneys**, lungs and liver may all still be carrying out the tasks for which they developed so many years earlier. However, not everyone is so lucky. **Organ systems** can be damaged in a number of ways, or may stop functioning altogether, for a number of reasons. The effect this has on the person concerned ranges from distressing – when, for example, the sight or the hearing is lost because of damage to the eyes or ears – through to completely life-threatening – for example when an organ such as the heart, liver or kidneys fail.

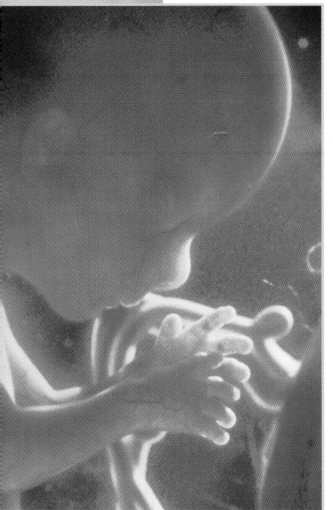

Problems can start even before a person is born. Sometimes organs do not form properly as the **embryo** develops. If the problem shows up on an ultrasound **scan** – a technique using very high frequency sound to see inside the body during pregnancy – then doctors and the parents are prepared. If surgery is possible, it is done shortly after the birth. Sometimes it can even take place while the baby is still developing in the **uterus**. Babies born after this type of surgery heal so well, they are born without a scar! But even with all the modern technology available

While a baby is developing in the uterus, many of its main body functions are dealt with by the mother's body, through the **placenta**. If its heart or lungs do not work properly it is not greatly affected. But after birth, the baby can be in real trouble – indeed babies die on a regular basis because of faulty organs that have failed to develop in the uterus.

today, babies are still born with unexpected organ problems. When this happens, the worst case is that the baby will die before surgery can correct the problem. However, in many cases, the child can be kept alive for at least a few weeks or months, by which time a solution – corrective surgery or a transplant – may be found.

Kidney infections

Sometimes people are born with a set of perfectly healthy organs, but develop an **infection** at some stage of their life that attacks and damages an organ beyond repair. For example, if an infection in the urethra (the tube which carries urine from the bladder out of the body) is neglected, the infection can spread up into the bladder and on into the kidneys, causing kidney damage and even kidney failure. Although many kidney infections are easily treated with antibiotics, repeated infections over the years or sudden very severe infections can both result in kidney failure. Without the kidneys, **urea** quickly builds up to **toxic** levels and the water balance of the body is lost. Death will occur a few days after the kidneys fail.

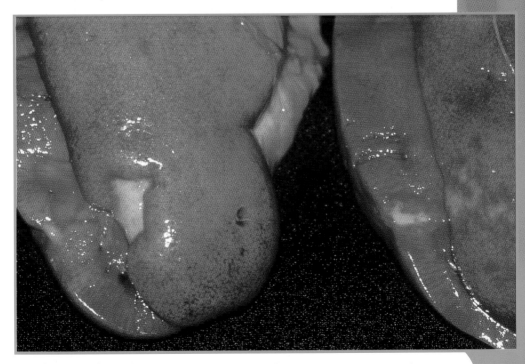

When an infection takes hold it can destroy an organ with terrifying speed. Within days, healthy kidney tissue can be damaged forever. This kidney has been damaged by a rapid bacterial infection.

Other infections

The kidneys are not the only organs that can be affected by the invasion of **micro-organisms**. Infections of the heart can damage the heart muscle so severely that it can no longer pump the blood effectively – and a badly damaged heart can cause death even more rapidly than failing kidneys. Similarly, hepatitis, a disease that is becoming increasingly common in the developed world, causes massive destruction of the liver cells. The same thing happens if the liver is attacked by liver **cancer**, another reason why liver function is sometimes lost.

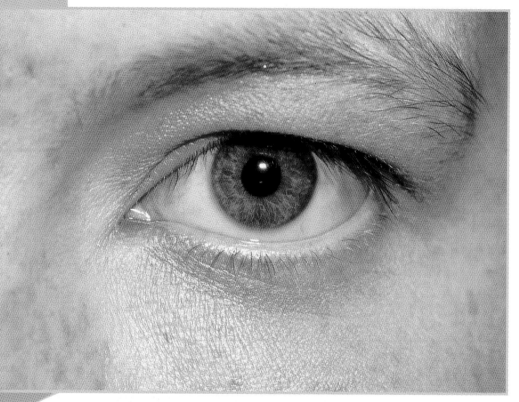

Typical symptoms of liver disease include a yellow skin and yellow 'whites' of the eyes. Bile, produced from the breakdown of the red blood cells, is not removed by the liver and builds up in the blood, colouring the skin and other **tissues**. In contrast to the skin, the faeces lack the colour of the bile pigments, and so appear very pale. This is known as jaundice, and the level of jaundice can give an immediate indication of how well the liver is working.

The gut too can be attacked by severe infections which damage the lining so badly that it can no longer absorb food, and it needs to be replaced. In the most severe infections, there is multiple organ failure. Even transplant surgery cannot help in these circumstances.

Gradual damage

Organ failure that results from severe infection does not always happen rapidly. Sometimes the destruction progresses relatively slowly, with the functioning of the organ getting weaker over a number of years. This can be caused by progressive illnesses or by damage caused by drugs. Drinking too much alcohol over a period of time can cause permanent liver damage – and brain damage as well. Smoking cigarettes causes damage to the lungs, damaging the structure of the delicate **air sacs** and making it harder and harder to get enough oxygen into the blood. It also affects the heart, making **heart attacks** more likely. If unsuitable drugs are given to a patient, kidney and liver damage can result. High blood pressure is another common cause of damage to organs such as the kidneys. Once the filtering mechanism is damaged the organs never work properly again.

> *'My kidneys started to fail when I was given a drug to treat another problem. For the first nine and a half years I coped by managing my diet very carefully – I could only eat small amounts of **protein** and the levels of liquid and salt I took in mattered, too. But eventually I became more and more tired and began to feel really unwell.'*
>
> Bernard Everard, a kidney patient, describing the gradual failing of his kidneys when he was in his fifties, after a prescribed drug for another illness caused irreversible kidney damage

Another common cause of organ damage occurs when the coronary arteries, the blood vessels that supply blood to the heart, become narrowed due to a build-up of fatty deposits on the walls. If a clot then forms in the blood and blocks the blood vessel, the muscle walls of the heart are starved of oxygen and may die. This is what is commonly known as a heart attack or coronary thrombosis. Even if the patient survives the attack, if the heart is severely damaged it may never work as effectively again.

So the organs of the body can fail for a number of reasons. Problems can arise at any time from **conception** onwards, although the risk of organ failure gets higher with age. But many babies and young children also face the prospect of a much shortened life if some of their vital organs begin to fail. The challenge is to find ways to repair or replace those failing organs and give the patients back their quality of life.

> *'One day Christopher was playing happily with the other children – and a few days later, his life was hanging in the balance and his kidneys had failed completely. The infection struck so quickly, we were all completely stunned.'*
>
> Ann Fullick, describing the speed at which a neighbour's child was affected by a kidney infection

New parts for old

For centuries, doctors have struggled to deal with the life-threatening situation of organ failure, and for most of that time there has been little or nothing they could do. Today, however, there are a number of ways of helping such patients not only to survive, but to live very healthy, active lives. One of the ways of restoring quality of life to a patient with failing organs is to give them an organ transplant.

The history of organ transplantation goes back a very long way. People recognized that if they could replace damaged or broken body parts, many other people would be healed. But progress was very slow because extremely sophisticated science needed to be unravelled before successful transplants could really become possible. In spite of this, some early attempts were made.

In 800 BC, there was a report in India that a surgeon called Susrata **grafted** new noses on to people using flaps of skin. From around AD 200 in China, there were reports of Hua-To replacing diseased organs with healthy ones. This seems unlikely because of what we now know about **rejection**, but if family members were used as **donors**, or a lucky **tissue** match came up, he could have had enough success to make an impression. Nobody says how long the patients lived!

But genuine transplants, where a new organ is placed in the body of the **recipient** and restores them to a healthy way of life, have been a long time in coming.

The compatibility question

Before transplants could help people overcome the problems of failing organs, scientists needed a better understanding of the human body. An important step was developing their knowledge of the human **immune system**. The basis of this system is the recognitive ability of cells. It can tell the difference between the cells of the person's body and all other cells. It therefore rejects and destroys transplanted organs because it recognizes them as different. This means that not only have scientists and doctors needed to develop surgical techniques for successful transplants, but they have also had to find ways

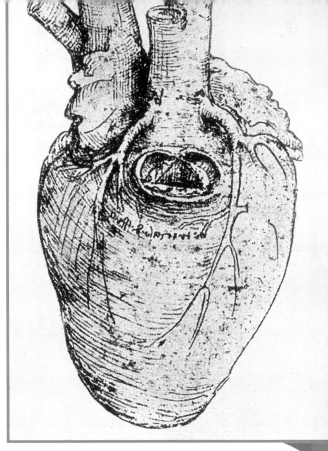

From very early times people tried to understand what was going on inside their bodies. However their knowledge was limited to what they could find out from examining dead bodies. Over the centuries many careful drawings of human organs were made, and understanding of the way organs worked grew, too. This drawing of the heart by Leonardo da Vinci dates from the fifteenth century.

(for example using special drugs) of preventing rejection of the new organ. Throughout the first 50 years of the last century, doctors and scientists were gaining in knowledge and understanding of how the organs of the body worked. They were also learning to recognize some of the signals used by the immune system. Sir Peter Medawar, often known as the father of modern immunology (the study of the immune system), did a great deal of pioneering work with skin grafts during World War II, leading to a far deeper understanding of the problems of rejection (for more on the immune system and the problems of rejection, see pages 28–29). Scientists and doctors were working towards the point where they would be able to transplant organs from one person to another, but this was always going to be an enormous leap in the dark. The patients would be very sick, indeed dying people – yet if the organ transplant failed to save them the technique would be seen as a failure.

Transplanting kidneys

Kidneys were the first organs to be transplanted successfully. During the early 1950s, a number of experimental kidney transplants were carried out in America and France, but they were largely unsuccessful. In 1954, the first successful kidney transplant was carried out by Dr Joseph E. Murray in Boston, USA. The donor was the living identical twin of the patient, which meant that there were no problems with rejection. The cells of identical twins are identical, so the immune system of the twin who received the donor kidney did not recognize the new kidney as different. The transplanted kidney worked for a further eight years.

Dr Joseph E. Murray won the Nobel Prize for Medicine in 1990, for his pioneering work on kidney transplantation. Of English and Irish origins, he began his surgical career in the USA, working on soldiers burned during WWII. This is where his interest in the problems of avoiding rejection began. His work on kidney transplantation helped make successful life after transplantation a reality for many thousands of people.

Then in 1959, Murray, working with his colleague Dr Merrill, performed a kidney allograft (graft from one person to another who is not genetically identical). In this case the donor and the recipient were also twins, but they were not identical. Another team, led by J. Hamburger in Paris, had similar success with another pair of twins. But another big hurdle still had to be overcome. Far more people needed new kidneys than there were donors – and not many people have a convenient identical twin. Could they use the kidneys from dead donors instead of live donors?

The pioneers – making transplants a reality

In 1962, the team in Boston, USA triumphed again – they transplanted a kidney from a dead donor into a live patient who was given drugs to try and prevent rejection. The new kidney worked successfully for 21 months before it was finally rejected by the body of its new owner. After this, developments came thick and fast. People were trying all sorts of methods to overcome the problems of rejection. Early methods included irradiating patients (exposing them to electro-magnetic radiation) before transplant surgery to destroy their **bone marrow**. This was to stop the production of **lymphocytes** (white blood cells), as these would attack the new organ. The problem with the irradiation method was that patients sometimes died as a result of it, as the transplant didn't have a chance to survive. Special anti-rejection drugs were also introduced. In the early days, these were very **toxic** and again, the anti-rejection treatment sometimes killed the patient.

In spite of the early difficulties, a floodgate had opened and new and different organ transplants were taking place every year. In 1963 the first human liver transplants took place at the University of Colorado, USA. They were carried out by Dr Thomas Starzl. However, the best survival time was only 21 days. That same year Dr James Hardy carried out the first lung transplant in Mississippi, USA. By 1966 the first successful transplant of a pancreas (an organ that makes hormones and digestive enzymes) from a dead donor had taken place. Starzl continued his work, and in 1967 his team performed the first really successful liver transplants, with four of their seven patients surviving for weeks and even months.

Building on success

Heart transplants became a reality in 1967, with the work of Christiaan Barnard. After this massive step forward, there was a period during which transplant surgeons and scientists working on rejection consolidated their work. Much research was done on improving operating techniques. Anti-rejection treatment also got better and patient survival times grew longer and longer.

Then, in the 1980s, things moved forward dramatically again. The first combined heart and lung transplant took place in 1981. It was carried out by Dr Norman Shumway and Dr Bruce Reitz at Stanford University, USA. Then, in 1988, Dr David Grant operating in Ontario, Canada achieved the first successful transplant of a small intestine. Since then, through the 1990s and on into the 21st century, great improvements have been made in anti-rejection drugs. This has meant that the chances of a transplant being rejected by the body of the recipient have been much reduced, and so transplant surgery has become increasingly successful.

There has also been an increase in the number of organs that it is possible to transplant at one time. Multiple-organ transplants, with up to four different donor organs being given to a single very sick patient, have become a reality – although they are still relatively rare. The most common organs to be transplanted in this way are the liver and various other abdominal organs, such as the small and large intestines.

The big one – transplanting hearts

The beating of the heart is so closely associated with life that it is almost impossible to imagine that someone could have their heart removed and survive the experience. Yet this is what happened in 1967, when Dr Christiaan Barnard in Cape Town, South Africa, carried out the first ever successful human heart transplant. The patient, a middle-aged man called Louis Washkansky, was given the heart of a young 23-year-old woman who had died in a car accident. The whole world was amazed at what had been achieved. Louis lived for eighteen days with his new heart beating in his chest before dying of a lung **infection**. A second attempt, by an American team in New York, failed – the patient died after six hours. But in 1968 Phillip Blaiberg received a new heart in the second transplant carried out by Dr Barnard, and he lived to enjoy a relatively normal life for nearly two years. Nowadays, heart transplant surgery hardly even makes local headlines.

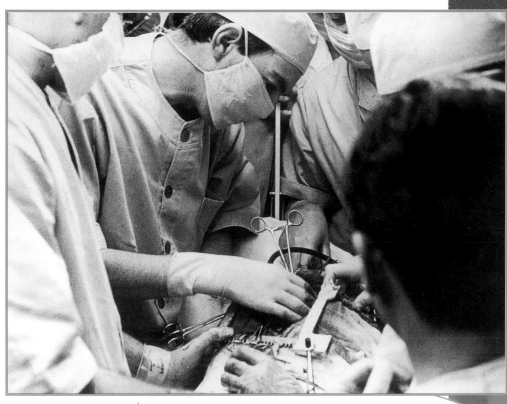

The pioneering work of people like Dr Joseph Murray (see page 16), Dr Thomas Starzl and Dr Christiaan Barnard paved the way for organ transplants to become a recognized way of treating patients with total organ failure. Dr Barnard is seen here carrying out an experimental operation on a dog. However it is important to remember patients such as Louis Washkansky (shown below) and Phillip Blaiberg and their families. Without their bravery and the enormous generosity of the bereaved families who donated organs, none of this progress would have been possible.

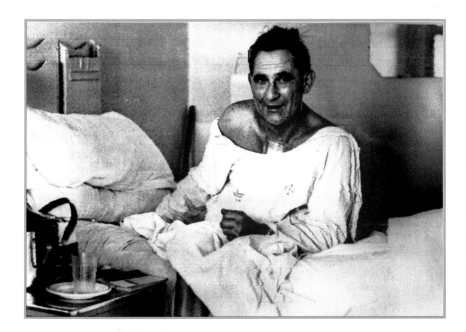

How is it done?

If a battery runs out in a toy, it is easily replaced. When a light bulb stops working, it takes just a few moments to remove the old bulb and put in a new one. When organs of the body fail for whatever reason, replacing them is not nearly so simple!

When a potential **donor** organ becomes available, there is a great deal to do. The **tissue** type of the donor must be matched as closely as possible with a person needing an organ transplant. There are two operating teams working at the same time, sometimes in the same hospital, sometimes in other parts of the country or even in another country. One team removes the organs from the body of the organ donor and packs them in specially prepared boxes for transporting to the operating theatre, where they are needed for a transplant. Meanwhile, the other team will be preparing the **recipient** to receive their new organ.

It is important that the donor organ is ready and waiting in the operating theatre before the recipient's diseased organ is removed. The organ may have to be transported hundreds of kilometres – and speed is of the essence!

Keeping organs fresh

It is vitally important that the donor organs are kept healthy and functional once they have been removed from the donor's body. This is done by washing the blood out of them using special, chilled preservation fluid, which produces a state of 'suspended animation' in the organ. This means the vital functions of the organ temporarily stop, but will return when the organ is connected to a bodily system again. They are stored in this fluid, surrounded by ice, to keep them at 4°C while they are transported to wherever they are needed. If ice actually came into contact with the tissue, it would freeze it and cause permanent damage, and the organ would be of no use.

The preservation fluids are very specialized. Research goes on all the time to improve them so that the organs can survive out of the body for longer periods of time. The fluids may cost as much as £150 per litre!

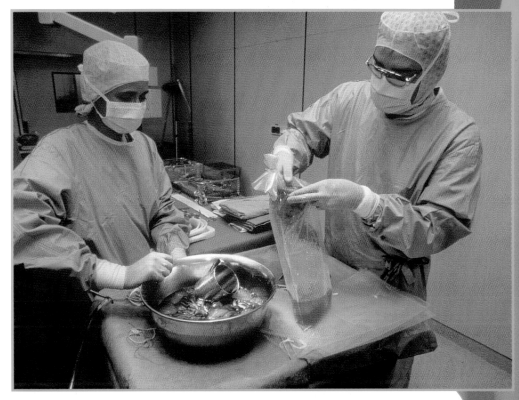

The specialized preservation fluid in which this kidney is being stored, along with low temperatures, will make sure it remains healthy while it is not functioning as part of a body.

The transplant operation

Transplanting organs always involves surgery, and all surgery involves some risk to the patient. Firstly, the patient needs to be under an anaesthetic, in a chemically induced sleep, while the operation takes place, so that he or she does not feel what is going on. It often takes a long time to carry out a transplant operation – several hours at least. The patient has to be carefully monitored to make sure there are no problems, and the risk of problems arising increases the longer the patient is under the anaesthetic.

Secondly, transplant surgery involves opening up the body to take out the old organ and replace it with a new one. As with all surgery, as soon as the body is opened up, it is very vulnerable to **infection**. Because transplant surgery goes on for a long time, and involves introducing an organ from someone else's body, the risk is increased.

Transplant challenges

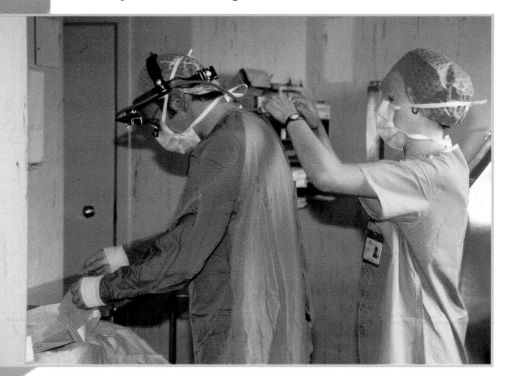

The operating team – surgeons, anaesthetists, theatre nurses and technicians – has to maintain incredibly high standards of cleanliness. This is to make sure that the site of the operation does not get infected while the patient is in the operating theatre. Again, this is like any other operation, but because transplants tend to be quite long operations, there is more opportunity for things to go wrong.

Transplanting an organ raises some particular challenges. Each organ in the body carries out specific and very important functions. In many operations, the body of the patient continues as normal whilst surgery on a particular part goes on. During a transplant, entire organs are removed, and so their function may have to be taken over by machines. This is particularly true in heart and lung transplants, because the body cannot function without the oxygen they provide. The patient is also often chilled, because at a low temperature the cells of the body need much less oxygen and sugar and they produce less waste. This means the cells are more likely to survive without any damage.

Another problem is making sure that the donor organ fits into the body of its new host. Obviously, transplants are only given when there will be a reasonable match between the size of the donor and the recipient, but even then there may still be problems. The original organ and the replacement will not be exactly the same, and neither will the blood vessels that supply them with blood. Yet these blood vessels have to be joined together in such a way that they won't leak. If the organ is much smaller or larger than the original, then this can cause problems. Once the bloodflow is allowed to return to the new organ, the doctors watch to see if the blood supply works and whether the transplanted organ seems to 'come alive' in its new body.

*'The most exciting thing when you are working as a transplant surgeon is when you have put the new **kidney** in the body. You take a small, brown, cold, insignificant little thing with all the blood washed out of it from the box. You put it into your patient, connect the blood vessels – and when you remove the clamps the whole organ turns pink and expands as new life flows into it. It never stops being amazing!'*

Anne M. Walters, consultant renal transplant surgeon,
Wessex Renal Transplant Unit, UK

Anne Walters (seated front centre) and her team at Portsmouth, UK, carry out kidney transplants – the most commonly performed transplants and the most successful.

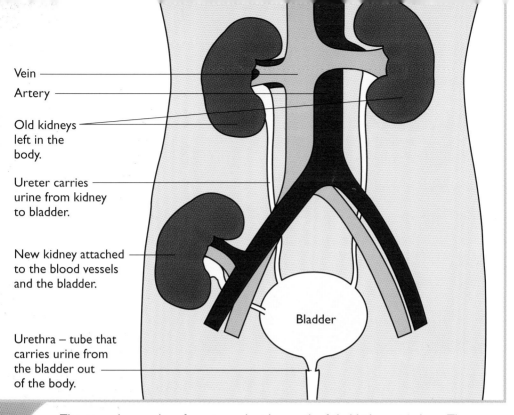

Vein

Artery

Old kidneys left in the body.

Ureter carries urine from kidney to bladder.

New kidney attached to the blood vessels and the bladder.

Urethra – tube that carries urine from the bladder out of the body.

Bladder

The normal procedure for a transplant leaves the failed kidneys in place. The new kidney is positioned lower in the body and the blood vessels of the kidney are connected to the blood vessels going to the legs, whilst the ureter, the tube from the kidney that carries urine away, is linked directly into the bladder.

Bigger and better

For many years, as transplant surgery was developed, single organs were transplanted to replace organs that had ceased to function. But over the years, transplant surgeons have developed a number of different techniques, some of which involve transplanting several organs at a time.

Sometimes transplants will be carried out when the patient's own organ still functions to a small extent. In these cases, 'piggy-back' transplants may be carried out. This means that a new organ is joined to the patient's own organ so that they work together. The new stronger organ carries out most of the work, allowing the original organ to rest and in some cases to recover. If it does, even if the 'new' organ is eventually **rejected** and has to be removed, the patient will remain healthy.

Doctors have become increasingly ambitious in the number of organs they transplant. Very often the failure of one organ leads to problems in another. For example, lung disease can cause damage to the heart, or problems in the liver can lead to failure of parts of the digestive system. There has been a gradual increase in the transplantation of more than one organ at a time. The first successful heart/lung transplant was carried out by Dr Norman Shumway and Dr Bruce Reitz at Stanford University, USA in 1981. Since then a number of different organ combinations have been transplanted successfully, including up to four different **abdominal organs** at a time!

'The day after I had my transplant, I couldn't believe the effect it had on my thought processes – it was as if a fog had been lifted off my mind.'

Ex-naval officer after receiving a new kidney

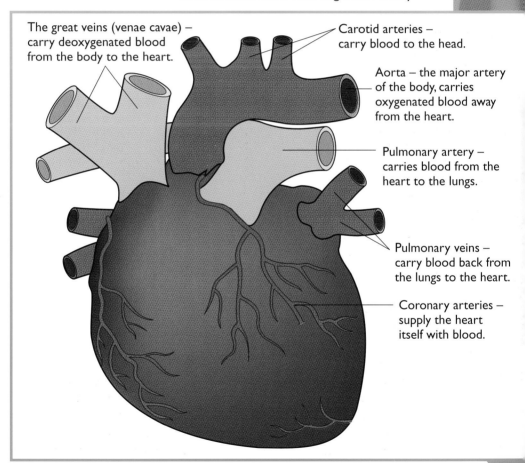

The great veins (venae cavae) – carry deoxygenated blood from the body to the heart.

Carotid arteries – carry blood to the head.

Aorta – the major artery of the body, carries oxygenated blood away from the heart.

Pulmonary artery – carries blood from the heart to the lungs.

Pulmonary veins – carry blood back from the lungs to the heart.

Coronary arteries – supply the heart itself with blood.

When a heart transplant is carried out, the failing heart is removed and the new organ placed in the chest cavity to replace it. All of the massive blood vessels carrying blood back to the heart from the body, and out around the body from the heart, have to be reconnected so that blood doesn't leak out and make the new organ inefficient.

Domino transplants

Another new type of transplant surgery was developed in the USA in 1987. Sometimes a patient has damaged lungs but a perfectly healthy heart – for example with **genetic diseases** such as cystic fibrosis. Although lung transplants can be carried out and are effective in these cases, often complete heart/lung transplants are more successful. This is because the connections between the heart and the lungs do not have to be made, and the two organs are the right size for each other. These transplants are known as a **domino transplants** because the healthy heart of the patient who receives the new heart and lungs is then transplanted into someone else who needs a new heart. Domino transplants are still relatively rare, but when they do take place they can be very successful.

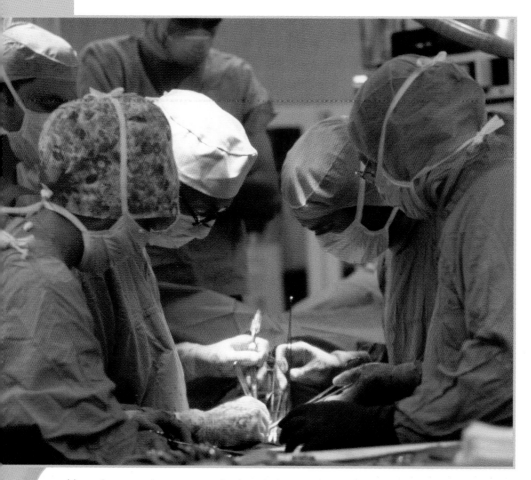

Here the transplant team at the hospital at Stanford University in California removes the diseased heart and the lungs from a patient.

Transplant co-ordinators

Whatever type of transplant is carried out, the success of the whole complex procedure depends heavily on the transplant co-ordinators.

Transplant co-ordinators, like Nicola Ashby (left) and Jill Pallister at the Wessex Renal Transplant Unit, UK carry out a number of roles, pulling together all the threads which keep a transplant unit running smoothly.

They are involved in supporting the recipient and their family as they prepare for the transplant, through the operation and afterwards as they recover and learn to manage the all important **immuno-suppressant** drugs. One of their most important jobs is co-ordinating the transplant process once a donor has been found. They make sure that everyone is in the right place at the right time and that the donor organ and the recipient are in a fit condition for the surgery to go ahead. They also work with the donor families, supporting them in their grief and helping them come to terms with events. The transplant co-ordinators continue their support for the donor families long after the various transplants have gone ahead. Not only this, they play an important role in educating family doctors, hospital doctors and the general public about transplant surgery.

Rejection!

There are many worries and problems for doctors involved in organ transplantation, and for the people who have received a transplant, whatever the type or number of organs received. But the biggest fear of all is that of **rejection** – when the patient's **immune system** begins to recognize the new life-giving organ as foreign and tries to destroy it. What is the immune system and why is it so important?

How the immune system works

The human body recognizes the presence of foreign antigens by means of lymphocytes. Everybody makes thousands of different lymphocytes and each lymphocyte recognizes one specific antigen. Lymphocytes involved in the immune response of the body are divided into two types – T-cells and B-cells. They are both made in the **bone marrow** and then move to different sites in the body and are divided into two types to grow and mature. The T-cells bind to foreign cells directly whilst the B-cells make antibodies. A single B-cell can make up to 2000 antibody molecules per second! Once the right antibody has been made, special memory cells make sure that if the body ever comes into contact with that foreign antigen again, it can respond immediately with the right antibody.

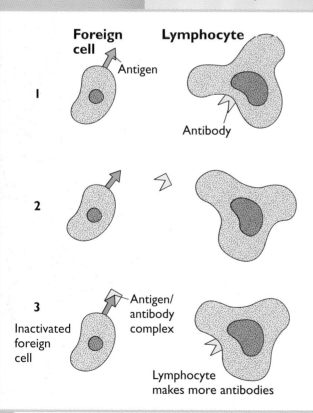

Foreign cell   **Lymphocyte**

Antigen

Antibody

1

2

3

Inactivated foreign cell

Antigen/ antibody complex

Lymphocyte makes more antibodies

The antigen/antibody reaction is a very clever way of making sure that the body recognizes foreign cells. However, because the antigens on the surface cells of a donor organ are different from those on the recipient's cells, the whole system backfires. In a transplant patient, the immune response can mean death rather than life.

The immune system

The immune system enables individual cells within the human body to recognize each other as part of the same living thing, and to recognize other cells which carry out the same jobs so they can work together as part of a **tissue** or an organ. It also recognizes foreign cells – invading **micro-organisms** such as bacteria and viruses which might cause disease, and transplanted organs – as 'non-self', which need to be destroyed.

How do cells recognize each other?

Sticking out from the surface of cell **membranes**, there are many special marker **molecules** known as **antigens**. Each individual person has some specialized antigens on the surface of their cells, which are unique to them. It is these individual markers that form the basis of the immune system and enable the body to recognize very rapidly if an organ from another person is placed inside it. Special white blood cells called **lymphocytes** make **proteins** called **antibodies**, which attach to any foreign antigens and inactivate the invading cells, which are then destroyed.

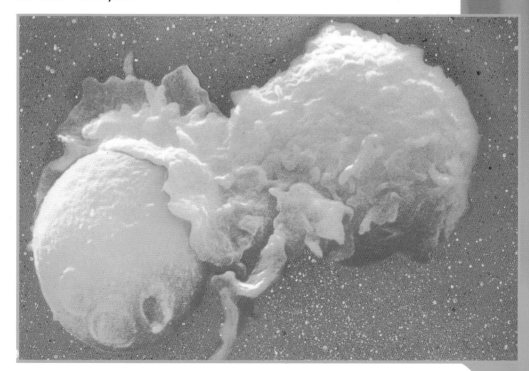

Once the lymphocytes have destroyed a foreign cell, phagocytes – another type of white blood cell – move in to engulf and 'eat' the dead cell. The phagocytes are the rubbish-collectors of the body and they move around clearing up after the lymphocytes. The pus you see in an infected cut is made up largely of dead phagocytes, which have taken in so many dead bacteria, it has killed them!

Human blood groups – another step forward

The human immune system is extremely complicated and makes life very difficult for doctors wanting to transplant organs from one person to another. For example, human beings have some unique antigens on their red blood cells, and this divides the population into different blood groups. If some blood groups are mixed together, the antigens react with antibodies in the blood, causing the cells to stick together. This blocks blood vessels and can kill a patient. However, other blood groups can be mixed with no ill-effects. This means that for any transplant to be successful, the blood groups of the **donor** and **recipient** must be the same or at least compatible. If not, the transplant is doomed to failure from the start. As the ABO system of categorizing human blood groups was not discovered until 1901, there wasn't much chance of successful transplant surgery before that time.

The immune system, which is so important in protecting the body against disease, is the worst enemy of a transplanted organ. The battle to prevent rejection has determined how successful transplant programmes have been. For many years the resources available to doctors were very limited and involved almost the total destruction of their patients' immune systems, leaving them open to a wide range of **infections**. Two advances have helped to weigh the odds more strongly in favour of the patient who has received a new organ.

Making a match

All people have some antigens in common. Others are specific to a particular individual. The more closely related two individuals are, the more likely they are to have lots of antigens in common. However, completely by chance, some unrelated individuals also have very similar sets of antigens. But the only people who have exactly the same antigens on their cells are identical twins, because they both came from the same **fertilized** egg and sperm.

As human understanding of the immune system has increased, so more and more care has been taken with matching the tissues between donor and recipient. The more similar the antigens on the donor organ are to the antigens on the cells of the recipient, the better the chances of the transplant 'taking' and rejection being avoided.

In the UK and Europe, there are computer data banks of the tissue type of all the people waiting for organs, and so when a donor becomes available, the most suitable recipients can be found. Organs are then transported at speed to where they are needed. Until recently, each state in the USA tended to use any available organs within that state. Relatively recent legislation has changed this so that organs are offered to the sickest people with the best tissue match, rather than to the nearest needy patient. Unfortunately for the patients, some states are contesting this in spite of the evidence that tissue-matching is important. US research has shown that out of 7614 people who got a perfect tissue-match transplant, 52 per cent of the organs were still working ten years later. In contrast, out of a group of 81,364 patients who had less than perfect matches, only 32 per cent of the organs were still working ten years later. So a good match makes a lot of difference.

Ensuring that recipients get tissue-matching organs often involves flights at speed across great distances to get the right organ to the right patient.

Preventing rejection using drugs

In 1969, scientists in America and Norway discovered a **fungus** that was to have far-reaching effects on the success of transplant surgery in the future. In 1972, Jean Borel, working in Switzerland, found that a chemical called **cyclosporine**, which could be isolated from the fungus, had **immuno-suppressant** properties – in other words, it damped down the reaction of the immune system. By 1980, this 'wonder-molecule' had been **synthesized** for the first time, and by 1983, it was approved for commercial and clinical use. When cyclosporine is given to patients after a transplant, the risk of rejection is greatly reduced because the activity of their immune system is lowered.

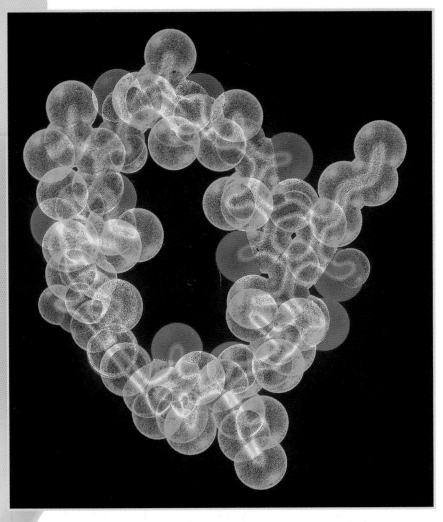

A computer model of a molecule of cyclosporine, the amazing new immuno-suppressant drug that has enabled thousands of people to benefit from an organ transplant without rejection problems.

Cyclosporine, particularly when used in partnership with other drugs such as some **steroids**, has had a major impact on the numbers of people having successful transplants. Transplant patients have to take their immuno-suppressant drugs for the rest of their lives, because the body would never get used to the new organ and accept it. The main downside of drugs like this is that they suppress the whole immune system, making the people taking them more vulnerable to normal **infections**. However, because everyone is aware of this, transplant patients are simply carefully monitored and given other medicines to help them if they develop an infectious illness.

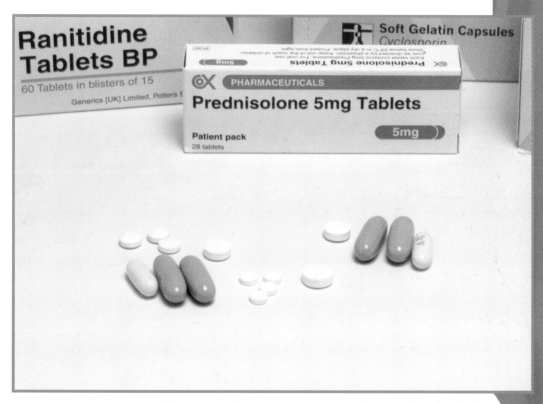

After a transplant operation, a patient has to take a cocktail of drugs every day for the rest of their life to prevent their immune system from destroying their new organ.

In the last ten years, many new drugs have been developed to help guard against rejection. Some replace cyclosporine, whilst others are used alongside it. Pharmacologists (people who study the science of drugs) are the great allies of transplant surgeons in the war against rejection!

Life from death

When someone has an organ that is failing, the obvious solution is to replace it with a new one. There is one huge problem with this, however – where is the new organ going to come from?

The most common source of **donor** organs are people who have died. Road accidents kill 3000 people a year in the UK alone. Many of those killed are relatively young and perfectly fit and healthy apart from the injuries – often to the brain – that kill them. Some people die from an unexpected haemorrhage (massive bleeding) in the brain, or a **heart attack**. Whenever a healthy person meets a sudden, unexpected death most of their organs will be in perfectly good condition. These organs can be given to someone else, someone who is dying because their heart, **kidneys**, liver or another organ can no longer fulfil its function.

Every day, people leave their homes to go to work, to school, out with friends – and never return. The roads claim many lives every week, and parents, children and partners have to come to terms with a sudden and totally unexpected loss.

Granting permission

A person who has suddenly died is obviously in no position to grant permission for their organs to be given to someone else. Yet without permission, it is illegal for doctors to remove organs from a dead body for the purpose of transplantation. What is more, if organs are to be used for transplantation, it is vital that the donor is kept on a life-support machine, so that even after they are clinically dead (all brain activity is lost), blood is pumped around their body and their organs are supplied with oxygen to keep them functioning. This is because if the body goes even a short time without oxygen, the organs will be damaged and therefore useless to anyone else. The machine takes over the functions of the heart and the lungs, getting oxygen into the blood, pumping it around the body and removing **carbon dioxide**.

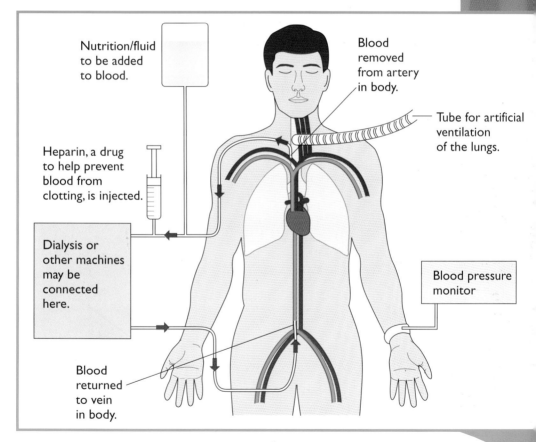

Nutrition/fluid to be added to blood.

Blood removed from artery in body.

Tube for artificial ventilation of the lungs.

Heparin, a drug to help prevent blood from clotting, is injected.

Dialysis or other machines may be connected here.

Blood pressure monitor

Blood returned to vein in body.

When an accident victim or someone who has suffered any type of medical catastrophe is brought into hospital, they will be put on a life-support machine if it is needed. This gives doctors the opportunity to assess the patient and see if there is any chance of his or her survival, and keeps the organs such as the liver and kidney functioning. If the patient's organs are to be used for transplantation, he or she will be kept on the machine even after they are found to be clinically dead, until the organs are removed.

When is death?

Doctors can only use a person's organs for transplantation if that person is dead – but how do we know when someone is dead and has no hope of recovery? In years gone by, people were judged to be dead when their heart stopped beating and they stopped breathing. Many people still think of death in this way. But in the case of sudden death, whether due to accidents or medical emergencies, machines can maintain the working of the body. In some cases, the heart keeps functioning at the level of a very basic reflex – a rapid nervous response that does not involve the **central nervous system**. In these cases, doctors have to look elsewhere for a definition of death. A patient is defined as being dead when their brain stem, the very lowest region of the brain, is dead. Once the basic regions of the brain stop functioning, the patient has no awareness, no thought, no life except that given by machines. Once a patient is certified as brain-stem dead – a process which takes a long time and several doctors – then the possibility of using the organs for transplantation becomes real.

A dreadful dilemma

When a patient is certified as dead, it is a terrible time for everyone concerned. Doctors are faced with a dreadful dilemma. If they ask the relatives – stunned, shocked, grieving – for permission to use the organs of their loved one for transplantation, then they may add to their distress. If they don't ask, then they are losing the chance of prolonging the lives of several people waiting desperately for an organ transplant. And, if the organs are to be used for successful transplants, there is no time to lose.

For the relatives, this is a hard decision to make at a dreadful time, and if they have not thought about it before, then they may feel unable to 'give away' part of their loved one's body. If the potential donor is on a life-support machine, then they will still be warm, appear to be breathing and will look as if they are simply asleep, making it even harder for relatives to accept that death has occurred. If permission to use the organs is refused, the life-support machine will be switched off when it seems right to the family – usually after a few hours.

The donor card

There is one thing that can make this situation easier for everyone concerned. In countries like the UK, the USA and Australia, there is a system of organ donor cards. Healthy, living people can decide that if anything should happen to them, then they would like their organs to be used to give life to other people. To show that this is their choice, they carry with them an organ donor card. If they are involved in an accident or taken seriously ill and die, the doctors know immediately that the organs are available for transplantation. Very often, people have also discussed this with their relatives, so that the family already know their wishes.

Donor Card

I would like to help someone to live after my death.

Let your relatives know your wishes and keep this card with you at all times.

I request that after my death
*A. my *kidneys, *corneas, *heart, *lungs, *liver, *pancreas be used for transplantation, or
*B. any part of my body be used for the treatment of others
* (DELETE AS APPROPRIATE)

Signature_____ Date_____

Full name_____
(BLOCK CAPITALS)
In the event of my death, if possible contact:

Name_____ Tel._____

The gift of life – if people are carrying organ donor cards when they die, doctors know that they can use their organs for transplantation and so have the greatest chance of making successful donations. In the USA, many states give people the option of having an organ donor card on the back of their driving licence, and in the UK, there is a computer database of registered organ donors who no longer need to carry a donor card.

Deciding to be a donor

When someone expresses a wish to be an organ donor after their death, it makes the situation so much easier if they do die suddenly. However, persuading people to become potential donors and carry a donor card is difficult. People often don't want to think about the possibility of their own death. Many other people are full of good intentions but simply don't get round to picking up a donor card. Some countries now have a system where everyone is automatically assumed to be a potential organ donor. Anyone who does not want to give their organs has to opt out of this system. This has greatly increased the number of organs available for transplantation in those countries where it has been tried, such as Belgium.

In many US states, it has been made law that doctors ask the families of all potential donors if they will allow donation. This means that they cannot be accused of insensitivity at a difficult time, because they are simply obeying the law. For many other families, however, the opportunity to donate organs from their loved one's body is seen as a way of bringing something positive out of a terrible situation.

'It is a very, very noble act – and human beings are capable of very noble acts... They can help seven or eight other people live who are about to die – they [the family] think that something good can come out of it.'
  Sir Magdi Yacoub, senior transplant surgeon at Harefield Hospital, UK

'If anything ever happens to me I want my organs to go to someone else.'
            Scott Dudley (US teenager), not long before he was killed in
          an accident with a gun. His organs gave two people their sight
          (using the corneas from his eyes) and four lives were saved
                    with his heart, kidneys, liver and pancreas.

Living donors

While most transplants are carried out using organs removed after death, not all organ donors are dead. Live donors are an increasingly important group. Most commonly, live donors are members of the same family as the person who is suffering from organ failure.

There is obviously a limit to the number and type of organs that can be given by a living donor. The most commonly donated organs are kidneys, because everyone has two of them. An individual can get on with life perfectly well with just one kidney, although they are obviously more at risk if they ever have kidney problems themselves –

Parents, brothers, sisters, uncles, aunts or cousins – blood relatives have a much higher chance of giving a very good tissue match than an unrelated donor. Husbands and wives have also sometimes been able to act as organ donors for each other. Here in Seattle, USA, Olufeyi Ogunyemi stands with her brother, who donated **bone marrow** to save her from sickle-cell anaemia.

they have lost their 'spare'. The liver, too, can be donated. Although each person has only one liver, it is a large organ that regrows at a very rapid rate. Part of the liver can be removed from a living donor, and blood vessels from this **tissue** joined to the blood vessels supplying the **recipient**'s liver. The liver tissue will regenerate in both the donor and the recipient very quickly, and the transplant will take over the function of the damaged or destroyed liver. On the other hand, organs such as the heart obviously cannot be given by a living donor, because everyone has only one heart and needs it to stay alive!

Most living donors give their organ freely either to someone they love or to someone they do not know but who has appealed for an organ as a matter of urgency. However, in some parts of the world where there is great poverty, such as India, there have been many instances of people selling their organs – particularly kidneys – for use in transplantation. Many groups find this unacceptable, particularly if people are pressured to do it. It seems wrong that people should compromise their own health simply for money.

Ethics and issues

When it comes to doing something as amazing as taking an organ out of one person – living or dead – and putting it inside the body of another person, there are bound to be all sorts of concerns associated with it.

Some people simply cannot come to terms with the idea of part of one person being used inside another, and feel that they could never be an organ donor. Other people find the idea of the body of someone they love being divided up and organs being removed very hard to accept, particularly if they only think about it when someone very close to them has died unexpectedly. Added to this, there are occasional 'scare stories' in the press of people taking on another personality after a transplant operation, particularly heart transplants. Other people feel that it would be against their religion.

In fact, most of the main religions have no problem with organ donation. The Christian religions all see organ donation, either from a dead or living donor, as an act of compassion and giving to save life. All churches share concern when the donor is dead, feeling that the body should be treated with respect, and that organ donation should not be done for money, but within these constraints, transplant surgery is seen as a good and beneficial form of medicine.

> 'Organ donation is an **altruistic** act which is motivated by compassion and a sense of social responsibility. Christians should, generally, be encouraged to reflect on how they can help those in need, even after death.'
>
> Right Reverend Michael Nazir-Ali, Bishop of Rochester

The teachings of Islam also support organ donation. Saving life is of paramount importance and Muslims are both allowed to accept organ donation and to act as organ donors themselves. Whilst in an ideal world both donor and recipient would be Muslim, in practice saving all life is seen as important.

> '…And if anyone saved a life it would be as if he saved the life of the whole people.'
>
> Qur'an, ch 5 v32

Many other religious groups also support transplantation – Hindus, Sikhs and Buddhists all see organ donation as being totally acceptable and more than that, a positive and generous gesture.

> 'Buddhists totally agree with organ donation. It is quite acceptable.'
> Ven Pidiville Piyatissa, Sri Lankan born Buddhist
> monk who has worked in the UK for eleven years.

Even the Jehovah's Witnesses, well known for their refusal to accept blood transfusions, are allowed to receive organ transplants if the surgery is carried out without the use of transfusions – and 'bloodless surgery' has been developed to allow this to take place. This involves chilling the whole body to very low temperatures to reduce any bleeding, and using special fluids which can carry oxygen to bathe the tissues, instead of blood products.

There is remarkable agreement from all religions about how right and unselfish organ donation is.

Lucy's story

Organ transplantation has always been an uncertain science. Even today, with all our knowledge and technology, transplants can fail immediately after they have been carried out or years later. This uncertainty is hard for doctors who cannot predict which transplants will be successful and which will not. It is much harder for the patients and their families, who have to live with that uncertainty every single day. The story of Lucy Sheehan shows what it is like to be on the receiving end of transplant surgery.

The first signs

On 11 December 1988, Amanda and James Sheehan welcomed their sixth child into the world. Lucy was an alert and endearing baby, but she stayed rather small – in fact she had regular medical check-ups because she was growing so slowly. However, by the time Lucy was two years old she was making up the lost ground rapidly, and her mother took her for what she hoped might be one of her last check-ups. Completely unexpectedly, Dr Ahmed Mukhtar felt that Lucy's liver was enlarged when he examined her, and decided to give her a **scan** just to make sure all was well. The results of the scan were frightening:

When Lucy (seen here on the left, with her older sister) was two, she appeared to be a normal, lively toddler. But she had to go into hospital and undergo a whole battery of tests to find out what was going on inside her liver.

Lucy's liver was fibrous and scarred – it looked as if she had **cirrhosis** of the liver, a disease that is more usually found in alcoholics!

The family was quickly referred to King's College Hospital in London, one of the top centres for research into liver disease in the UK and Europe.

> 'Most children with liver disease look ill and yellow – they have jaundice – but Lucy didn't, she didn't look ill at all. That made it very hard for us to believe that anything was wrong with her – it was all such a shock.'
> Amanda Sheehan, Lucy's mum

The whole process of going to hospital and having tests distressed Lucy greatly, but the results that came back showed that the scan had been right. Lucy really did have cirrhosis of the liver, but the doctors simply didn't know why. Somewhere the complex chemistry taking place in Lucy's liver had gone wrong, but in a way that had never been seen before. Because Lucy was still feeling so well, they decided that the best thing to do was keep a watching brief. Amanda and James were told to take her home and bring her along for regular check-ups every three months.

Lucy with a doctor from King's College Hospital in 1992. Although the Sheehan family didn't know it when they first took Lucy for liver tests, this famous hospital was going to play a major part in their lives for many years to come.

A grim reality

Once Lucy came back from her tests, life began to return to normal in the Sheehan family. With six children – Penny, Philip, Oliver, Nicholas, Hannah and Lucy – life was pretty hectic and there wasn't much time to brood about what might happen at the next check-up. But it was only two weeks later when the consultant rang Amanda with very bad news. More results from Lucy's tests had shown something 'abnormal'. Could they come back to the hospital as soon as possible? The doctors suspected that Lucy might have **cancer** of the liver, but it took more time and more tests before they could be sure. By the summer, when she was two and a half, the doctors finally arrived at a diagnosis. Lucy not only had cirrhosis of the liver, she also had cells that were pre-cancerous (becoming cancerous) and she needed a liver transplant as soon as possible. The longer she waited, the more likely it was that cancer would develop and spread beyond the liver. Without a transplant the doctors said she had about two years to live. In September 1991, Lucy officially went on the list of children waiting for a liver transplant.

> 'It was like being on a terrifying emotional roller coaster ride. We never knew what we would have to deal with next. To be told that your two year old child might not live to be four – we just went completely cold...'
>
> Amanda Sheehan, Lucy's mum

The long wait

Ideally, Lucy needed a transplant straight away – but **donor** organs are not simply available when they are needed. Yet the family knew that all the time they waited, Lucy's chances of survival were ebbing away. The constant round of hospital visits were taking a toll on everyone. James, Lucy's dad, ran the family business – so every time he took time off he wasn't earning money. And Lucy's brothers and sisters needed time and attention, too. The family had to pay someone to help look after the other children when Lucy and her mum made their many trips to the hospital.

Lucy's illness was affecting the whole family. Six children need a lot of looking after, and running a household for eight people takes a lot of money, especially when paying for extra help. All of the children were worried, and missed their mum and Lucy whenever they were away at the hospital. There was no sign of a donor organ becoming available, so when Amanda had the opportunity to appear on national television she grasped it and made an appeal for people to think about donating organs if their loved ones died.

Amanda and Lucy appeared on several television programmes where Amanda appealed for donor organs to be made available and helped explain what stresses this situation places on the whole family. Here they are on 11 June 1992 on TV-AM. Lucy received her transplant two days later.

As a result of their television appearance the family received a lot of support – people ran in marathons and organized collections to help them financially. Even more importantly, a couple of weeks later they received a call from the hospital to say a donor organ was available. Lucy was prepared for surgery, and the family all said goodbye. However, they knew that another little girl, even more poorly than Lucy, was also being prepared for surgery. The surgeons opened her up first. If she had cancer and it had spread, it would not have been worth transplanting the donor liver into her body. However, although her liver was cancerous, there was no sign of the disease spreading. Her need was greater and so she got the liver. Lucy and her family continued to wait.

The transplant

More time went by without an organ becoming available. After eight months, Amanda and Lucy went on television again to raise the profile of people needing transplants and to ask people to think about becoming organ donors. In that week alone, as a direct result of the TV appeal, enough donor organs were made available to enable nine children to have transplant operations. One of those children was Lucy.

On 13 June 1992, as the family was having a party to celebrate Hannah's birthday, the call came through to say a donor organ had been found. The whole family piled into the car and drove to King's College Hospital, with Lucy still in her party dress. Her brothers and sisters all said goodbye to her that night, knowing they might not see her alive again. On 14 June, the operation went ahead. James took the other children home, while Amanda waited at the hospital for the eight hours that Lucy was in the operating theatre. Lucy was given one lobe (section) of the liver of an older child – the liver normally consists of two lobes.

When Lucy emerged from the theatre, she was put into intensive care, but she only stayed there for 24 hours – she was soon pulling the ventilation tubes out! At three and a half Lucy couldn't really understand why she had come to hospital feeling fine and now felt so very poorly. For several weeks she refused to eat and had to be fed through a tube. She needed nine different medicines daily to prevent her body rejecting the new liver. After six weeks in hospital she went home, only to have her body start to reject the liver. Shaking, with a high temperature, she was rushed back into hospital as an emergency. The doctors were not surprised – most children who receive a new organ react like this. But once the **rejection** was under control, Lucy went home again and this time she recovered well, eating normally and getting back her zest for life.

The intervals between her check-ups got longer and longer as her new liver continued to work well. It wasn't all plain sailing, though. In the first two years after her transplant, Lucy had a number of **infections**, including glandular fever, a viral disease which attacks the glands of the **immune system** and causes extreme tiredness. The fever caused major problems because of the **immuno-suppressant** drugs she had to take – but Lucy and her family just kept going and their persistence paid off. Lucy is still fit and well today.

The liver that saved Lucy's life was donated by the family of a twelve-year-old boy who died during an operation on a tumour (an uncontrolled growth of cells) in his brain. No one had expected him to die, and doctors did not ask his stunned parents for permission to use their son's organs. It was the parents themselves who volunteered their son as a donor, in the midst of their own devastation. Their generosity allowed Lucy to live.

> *'I'm so grateful to my donor. My liver doesn't feel different or strange – it just feels like part of me. I feel completely normal.'*
>
> Lucy Sheehan, transplant patient

Lucy Sheehan is now a fit, active teenager. She has had her new liver for nine years and only has to take a very low dose of two medicines – including **cyclosporine** – each day. She goes to school and joins in all the same activities as her friends and relatives. She is a real transplant success story.

Pushing the boundaries

Every 27 minutes, someone somewhere in the world receives an organ transplant. But every two hours 24 minutes, someone dies, waiting for an organ **donor** to turn up. There are simply not enough donor organs available for all the people who need them, and if anything the problem is getting worse rather than better. As surgical techniques and **immuno-suppressant** drugs have improved, transplant surgery is seen as the answer to more and more medical problems. At the same time, the introduction of laws about the wearing of seat belts, a reduction in drinking and driving and improved car safety standards means fewer people are being killed in road accidents. Doctors are able to save the lives of more people who are rushed into hospital. These improvements are welcomed by everyone, but the inevitable side-effect is a reduction in the pool of potential organ donors.

Organs are released from only about 20 per cent of potential donors. Whatever is done to raise people's awareness of the importance of organ transplantation and the need for donors, the supply of donor organs from people who have died will never match the number of people needing transplants. Living donors are being used increasingly, but they too are a very limited resource. It is because of this mismatch of supply and demand that research has been going on into alternative ways of providing organs for transplantation.

Xenotransplantation

One area of research which has received a great deal of media attention and funding is **xenotransplantation**. This is the transplantation into people of organs from other species of animals. Xenotransplantation is not actually a new science. In 1906, a French surgeon, Mathieu Jaboulay, implanted a pig's **kidney** into one woman and a goat's liver into another. Both women died. But in recent years scientists began to think that the use of xenotransplants could solve two of the biggest problems of transplant surgery – the shortage of donor organs and the problems of **rejection**.

Most of the research into using animals as a source of organs for human transplants has been done using baboons and pigs. In 1964, six patients received baboon kidneys; in 1984, a baboon heart was transplanted into a baby girl; in 1992, two patients received baboon livers. All of the patients died within weeks of their operations, but they did not die because they had rejected their new organ. The high dosages of immuno-suppressant drugs they needed to take left them highly vulnerable to **infections**, and they died of these. However, baboons are not an ideal source of organs because they reproduce very slowly, having only one baby at a time. They also carry many viruses that could be passed on to the human **recipient**. When animals are used as a source of organs for human transplants, the animals are always killed. Because baboons are so similar to humans, both in the way they look and behave and in their biology, many people have **ethical** objections to using them as 'donors' in this way.

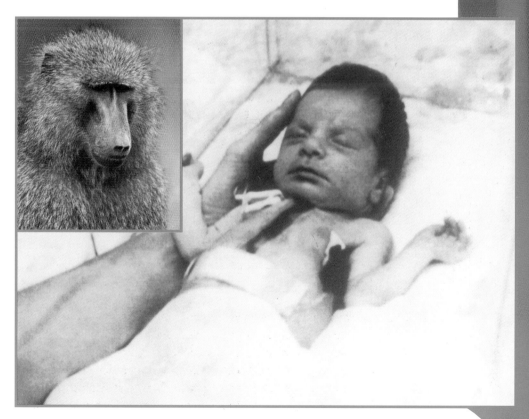

Baboons are genetically very close to human beings, so the idea was that rejection problems would probably be relatively small. Physically, too, the organs would fit easily into a person. In 1984 this little girl, known in the media as 'Baby Faye', received a baboon's heart to try and keep her alive. The baboon's heart worked in her body for 20 days, but she died of infection before a suitable human donor was found.

What about a pig's heart?

As potential organ sources, pigs have been the main focus of research. Despite the difference in body shape, the anatomy of a pig is amazingly like that of a human. They carry fewer viruses than baboons, and are much easier to breed, producing lots of piglets in each litter. Moral objections to using pigs are also fewer because they are killed for food anyway. The hope among researchers is that, using the techniques of **genetic engineering**, pigs may be modified so they produce hearts, livers, kidneys and other organs that carry neutral human **antigens**. This would mean the new organs would not be recognized by the human recipient as foreign **tissue**. The hope is that genetically modified pigs grown in a sterile environment might provide a virtually unlimited supply of disease-free 'human' organs for transplants, and that the recipients would need little or no immuno-suppressant drugs, as the new organs would be recognized by their **immune system** as 'self'.

Genetically modified pigs to be used for organ transplants would not be able to live in a natural environment like this. They would need to be reared in a very sterile, bio-medical environment – and this raises animal welfare issues. Would it be fair to treat these intelligent animals in this way?

Advantages and disadvantages

What are the big advantages of using animals to provide organs for human beings? Patients need never again die waiting for a donor organ. There would always be suitable organs available, and the problem of rejection could be removed. It sounds a wonderful solution to the problem – so what are the drawbacks of xenotransplantation? There are a number of ethical objections, not least because animals cannot give consent for the use of their organs, so they cannot be referred to as donors – they are organ sources. Also, the animals would have to be kept in very unnatural, sterile conditions.

The other major problem is the risk of disease. Like all animals, including ourselves, baboons and pigs carry a wide range of viruses – although pigs have fewer than baboons. Many of these are relatively harmless in the baboon or the pig, but any of them could cause a fatal disease in a human host. An example is the virus that causes **AIDS** – a relatively harmless virus in monkeys that has devastating effects in people. No one knows if xenotransplants would bring new and deadly diseases into the human race – but it is a very big risk to take.

'The potential for infectious agents to be passed from the source animal, via the transplant, to a human recipient and from the patient into the wider population is still a major concern… Until such time as research is able to produce more definitive answers on safety…it is prudent to assume that all forms of xenotransplantation carry a risk of some degree.'

Third annual report of the UK Xenotransplantation
Interim Regulatory Authority

A large amount of money has been ploughed into research on xenotransplantation, and pigs carrying human genes have been bred in the UK and elsewhere. However, the feeling increasingly seems to be that this will not be the answer, that there are too many problems to be overcome in xenotransplantation and that other areas of research will come up with the best solution for the shortage of donor organs.

'There has been a lot of scientific hype, leading people to believe that successful animal transplants are just around the corner. But now the regulator is saying that this is not the case and there are serious concerns about safety…'

Sarah Kite, British Union for the Abolition of Vivisection

Research – the cutting edge

The number of people waiting for an organ transplant around the world is large, and it is growing. About 44,000 Americans are on the waiting lists, yet only 18,270 operations were carried out in the year 2000. In the UK, there are almost 7000 people waiting for transplants, and in Australia the numbers are similar. It was hoped that **xenotransplantation** (see pages 48–49) would provide a ready supply of organs, but at the same time as those hopes faded, new discoveries were being made that may well be the answer to the organ shortage in the future.

The pluripotent stem cell

Stem cells divide and form the specialized cells of the body that make up the various **tissues** and organs. When an egg and sperm fuse to form an **embryo**, those early cells will eventually give rise to every type of cell in the adult human body. By the stage at which the embryo implants in the mother's **uterus**, it has become a hollow ball of cells. The inner cells of this ball are what is known as pluripotent – they will eventually form most, but not all, of the baby's cells. These pluripotent stem cells get

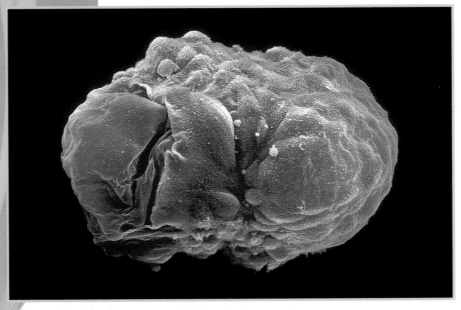

This is a very early human embryo. In the right conditions in the uterus these few cells can form all of the organs of the human body. Now scientists may be able to harness and use that potential.

even more specialized as the embryo develops, forming, for example, blood stem cells, which give rise to blood cells, and skin stem cells, which give rise to skin cells.

In 1998, in a breakthrough that caused ripples of excitement through the scientific and medical world, two American scientists managed to **culture** human embryonic stem cells that were still pluripotent. James Thomson and his research team at the University of Wisconsin maintained a culture of human embryonic stem cells for several months. They originally got the cells from spare embryos that had been produced during *in vitro* **fertilization** treatments. Couples had donated their spare embryos for scientific research, rather than simply having them destroyed.

At the same time, John Gearhart and his group at Johns Hopkins University were also culturing human embryonic stem cells, from a slightly different part of the embryo. The cells used by John Gearhart came from fetuses that had been aborted after five to nine weeks of development.

John Gearhart and his team, working at Johns Hopkins University, published their results on embryonic stem cells just four days after Thomson, and the two groups are both credited with this ground-breaking discovery.

Why so much excitement?

The culturing of embryonic stem cells has caused a major stir. In theory at least, the pluripotent cells could be encouraged to grow into almost any different type of cell needed in the body. They could provide an amazing variety of cures for diseases and other medical problems. For example, they could provide new nerve cells for people with brain disorders or spinal injuries, new heart muscle cells to repair hearts damaged by **heart attacks**, and new and effective treatments for **strokes**, burns and **arthritis**. For those people waiting desperately for a transplant, the hope is that it may be possible to produce whole new organs by growing the stem cells in the right conditions. This means there may be a potentially limitless source of **donor** organs. It could also revolutionize the treatment of many other diseases and change the testing of drugs, reducing the need for animal experiments.

At the moment, no one is quite sure just how the cells in an embryo are switched on or off to form particular types of tissue – **kidney** rather than liver, or liver rather than heart. As the answers to these questions are found, the potential will be there for a limitless supply of new organs. Not only that, but the problem of rejection could be solved. The **immune system** does not attack and destroy a developing embryo, even though it has different **antigens** on its cells to the mother. Perhaps new cells or organs created from embryo stem cells will enjoy this same protection.

The ethical stumbling block

The major **ethical** problem with research into pluripotent cells is that these cells come either from aborted embryos or from 'spare' embryos in fertility treatment. There are many people, including many religious groups, who feel it is wrong to use a potential human being as a source of material in this way. It is also argued that the embryo cannot give permission, so it is a violation of the embryo's human rights to use it.

The research is so controversial that funding was stopped for a time in the USA until the situation had been discussed in detail. Eventually the US government decided that from August 2000 such work could continue on human pluripotent cells obtained from aborted fetal tissue or from frozen embryos created during fertility treatment. There was also considerable debate in the UK before legislation was passed to extend the Human Fertilisation and Embryology Act to allow embryonic stem cell research to take place.

The use of embryonic stem cells from the umbilical cord (the cord that joins the developing baby to the mother's **placenta** in the uterus) may help to overcome some of the reservations. It may become possible to store stem cells from every newborn baby, so the cells could be used if the baby should need them later in life.

Scientists are also finding some stem cells in adults that appear to have the ability to grow into several different types of tissue. There seem to be more limitations with adult stem cells than with embryonic ones, because the adult stem cells found so far are limited in the cell types they can develop into. However, this is another possible way forward that could avoid both **rejection** problems and the controversial use of embryonic tissue.

Most people remain excited by the possibilities of embryonic stem cells in transplantation and other areas. Just how many of these early hopes will be fulfilled, only time will tell.

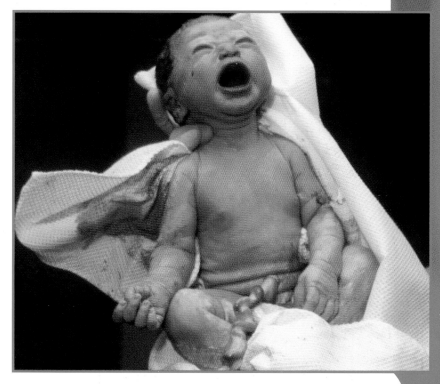

It may be possible to harvest embryonic stem cells from the umbilical cords of new born babies. This would avoid the use of tissue from early embryos and overcome ethical problems.

Into the future

The field of organ transplantation is an exciting and ever-moving one. Surgeons are continually looking for new techniques that will make transplants more effective and enable more organs to be transplanted. For example, the use of parts of both lungs and livers in transplants has made it easier to use live **donors**, and has meant that more people can be helped by a single dead donor.

Drug companies are working towards new drugs to help with the problem of **rejection**. In particular, they are trying to develop drugs that suppress the part of the **immune system** that causes the rejection of a transplanted organ without suppressing the body's natural defence against disease. The 'ideal scenario' of all transplant research is to develop rejection-free transplants.

Although there are constant innovations, not all of them are successful. In the 1970s, Robert Jarvik designed an artificial heart that he hoped would be able to function long-term in the human body, removing the need for human donors and avoiding problems of rejection. A number of these artificial hearts were transplanted and one patient, William Schroeder, lived for 620 days. However, the quality of life for these patients was not very good, and they suffered many **infections** and other problems. Eventually, doctors decided that the only real use for artificial hearts was to provide a bridge to a human transplant, prolonging a patient's life in the hope that a suitable donor might be found.

In the year 2000, the British surgeon Stephen Westaby in Oxford, UK, implanted a much smaller device, the Jarvik 2000, into the left ventricle (pumping chamber) of a patient's heart. This supported the function of the failing heart, helping to pump the blood effectively around the body, and the patient lived another five months. Since then, more implants like these have taken place. The hope for the future is that a tiny implant will replace the need for a full heart transplant.

How far can we go?

The idea of transplant surgery has grown and developed from a very experimental science in the last century to a well accepted treatment for many different forms of organ failure today. There are still problems that transplantation cannot overcome. If someone is severely brain damaged in an accident, such that their brain stem dies, their organs can be used to offer hope of new life to others – but the process cannot be reversed. Doctors cannot transplant a new brain and restore life within the damaged body.

However, there are many ways in which transplant medicine is a triumph of human endeavour. It can be used to help people of all ages. Tiny babies, children, teenagers, adults – even relatively elderly people in their seventies – have been given new **kidneys** and other organs that have restored their quality of life. Nothing can ease the loss of a loved one for donor families, but they do have the knowledge that their relative has helped others to live. Taking a dying person and restoring them to health using the organs of another person seems almost unbelievable – organ transplantation is a modern miracle of medicine.

'Carrying a donor card is rather like carrying a credit card, except that you are offering other people the chance of life. I wish everyone would carry one.'
Lucy Sheehan, successful transplant patient

When people have received a successful transplant, they can return to health and fitness. In many countries, transplant patients get together to compete in a whole range of different sports. In the British Transplant Games, all the competitors – up to a thousand of them – have received a transplant of some sort!

Timeline

800 BC   Susrata, a surgeon in India, is reputed to have **grafted** new noses from skin flaps.

AD 200   The first recorded reference to the concept of organ transplantation is made around this time – Hua-To in China is reported to have replaced diseased organs with healthy ones.

1902   The first successful **kidney** transplant (in a dog) is carried out by Emerich Ullman.

1940s   Sir Peter Medawar and others begin to understand and explain the human **immune system**.

1954   The first successful human kidney transplant takes place in the USA between identical twin brothers. The transplanted kidney works for eight years.

1959   Doctors Murray and Merrill carry out the first successful human kidney allograft between non-identical twins.

1962   The first successful kidney transplant using a dead **donor** is carried out in the USA. The kidney functions for 21 months.

1963   The first lung transplant is carried out by Dr James Hardy in the USA.

              Bone marrow is transplanted for the first time, leading to revolution in the treatment of **cancers** such as leukemia.

1966   A successful pancreas transplant is carried out for the first time in the USA.

1967   The first really successful liver transplant is carried out by Dr Thomas Starzl in the USA. The liver functions for thirteen months.

              The first successful human heart transplant is carried out by Dr Christiaan Barnard in South Africa. The heart functions for eighteen days.

1969   The **fungus** *Beauveria nivea* is discovered, which leads to the finding of **cyclosporine** in the USA and Norway.

1972	Jean Borel discovers the **immuno-suppressant** properties of cyclosporine.
1980	Cyclosporine is first **synthesized**.
1981	The first successful heart/lung transplant takes place in the USA. The new organs function for five years.
1982	The first artificial heart, the Jarvik 7, is transplanted into Barney Clarke.
1983	Cyclosporine is approved for use as an immuno-suppresant drug.
1984	'Baby Faye' in the USA is given a baboon's heart, which works for 20 days.
1987	The first **domino transplant** takes place.
	Dr Starzl is involved in the first successful transplant of several different **abdominal organs**.
1989	The first successful liver transplant from a living relative takes place in the USA.
	The first transplant of a complete small intestine.
1992	The first baboon to human liver transplant is carried out in the USA. The **recipient** lives for 70 days.
	First pig to human liver transplant. The recipient dies after two days.
1996	The first successful split-liver transplants take place – using the liver from a dead donor to give more than one recipient the chance of life.
1998	Human embryonic stem cells are **cultured** in the laboratory for the first time in the USA.
2000	The second Jarvik artificial heart (Jarvik 2000) is first used. The patient lives for five months.

Glossary

abdominal organs organs found in the abdomen, for example the digestive system and the kidneys

AIDS (acquired immune deficiency syndrome) condition caused by the HIV virus in which the immune system is severely weakened, leaving the patient vulnerable to diseases such as pneumonia and tuberculosis, from which the patient eventually dies

air sacs tiny spaces in the lungs where gas exchange takes place

altruistic unselfish towards other people

antibodies special proteins made by the immune system that attach to any foreign antigens and inactivate the invading cell

antigens special marker molecules sticking out from the surface of cell membranes

arthritis inflammation of the joints, a condition which is often very painful and can be crippling

bone marrow soft tissue in the hollow sections of the bones where blood is made

cancer potentially fatal disease caused by the uncontrolled growth of cells

carbohydrates type of food molecule that acts as an energy source

carbon dioxide gas produced as a waste product of respiration by most living organisms

central nervous system linked system of nerves, including the brain and spinal cord, which carry electrical messages around the body

cholesterol type of fat that is present in most body tissues. It is thought to be involved in many forms of heart disease.

cirrhosis disease of the liver, often caused by excess alcohol intake, where the liver function is progressively lost due to fibrous tissues replacing normal liver cells

conception moment at which a sperm and an egg join together to create an embryo

culture to grow micro-organisms or cells in the laboratory

cyclosporine drug that damps down the reaction of the immune system to foreign cells

domino transplants transplants that have a 'knock-on' effect, providing organs for two recipients. A patient with diseased lungs but a healthy heart receives a heart/lung transplant, and their healthy heart is then donated to a patient needing a heart transplant.

donor someone who donates an organ (either when they are alive, or promised after their death) to help someone who lacks this organ

embryo very early stages of human development in the uterus

ethical relating to what is morally right

fertilize to join a male and female sex cell together to form a new individual

fungus type of organism that produces spores, includes moulds, yeast and mushrooms

genetic diseases diseases that occur because of defects in the genes or chromosomes

genetic engineering process by which the genetic material of a cell may be altered either by replacing damaged genetic material or adding extra genetic material

graft to transplant a piece of tissue from one place on a person's body to another place, either on the same body or someone else's

heart attack when blood flow to the heart is reduced due to a blockage in the blood vessel, causing a sudden abnormality in the functioning of the heart

immune system system in the body that recognizes foreign cells and destroys them

immuno-suppressant causing a reduction in the activity of the immune system

in vitro **fertilization** medical treatment in which an egg is fertilized outside of the body of the mother before being returned to her uterus

infection invasion of the body by micro-organisms

kidney organ which removes waste urea and excess salt from the blood, producing urine which is passed into the bladder

lymphocytes white blood cells that make antibodies

membrane thin layer or 'skin' around cells

micro-organisms organisms, like bacteria, which are too small to see with the naked eye and need to be viewed through a microscope

molecule tiny particle, made up of more than one atom joined together

organ systems collection of organs working together to carry out a major function in the body

placenta organ in the mother's uterus that supplies a developing baby with food and oxygen

protein type of food molecule important for muscle-building and growth

recipient patient who receives a donated organ

rejection to refuse to accept; rejection of transplanted organs occurs when the body realizes they are not its own

scan way of looking into the body without opening it up. There are many different types of scan used by doctors in the diagnosis of disease and monitoring of health.

steroids lipid-based chemical. Some hormones are steroids and steroid drugs are used for a variety of reasons.

strokes sudden interruption of the brain's blood supply caused by the rupture of a blood vessel or a clot formation in the brain. These can damage the body's functioning and even cause death.

synthesize to make. Chemicals can be made artificially rather than extracted from a source (for example an organism).

tissue collection of cells in the body that all carry out the same function – for example muscle tissue

toxin (**toxic**) a poison (something that is poisonous)

urea toxic chemical made when excess protein is broken down in the body

uterus female organ in which the fetus develops

xenotransplantation transplanting an organ from one species of animal into another completely different species

Sources of information

Further reading

Heinemann Advanced Science: Biology, Ann Fullick (Heinemann Educational, 2000)
Human Health and Disease, Ann Fullick (Heinemann Educational, 1998)
Science Topics: The Human Body, Ann Fullick (Heinemann Library, 1999)
The Dorling Kindersley Science Encyclopedia, (Dorling Kindersley, 1998)
The Kingfisher Science Encyclopedia, Charles Taylor ed. (Kingfisher, 2000)

Websites

www.chron.com/content/chronicle/special/
transplant/history.html (Houston Chronicle)
This link gives a timeline of transplant history from 1933 to 1986. During these years the major breakthroughs in human transplantation were made, including the transplantation of kidneys, livers and hearts. The introduction of drugs that helped patients to retain transplanted organs and the establishment of national databases of donors also figure in this chart of transplantation developments.

www.med.umich.edu/1libr/heart/surg02.htm
(University of Michigan)
Heart transplantation is explained here. Information is given on who receives a heart transplant, how it is done and the complications of rejection.

www.med.umich.edu/1libr/topics/surg18.htm
(University of Michigan)
Following this link will take you to an explanation of organ and tissue donation. Features of the web page are the importance of donation, the criteria that donors must fulfil and a list of what parts of the body can be used.

www.transweb.org/reference/timeline/historytable.htm
(TransWeb)
Here you can find a global history of transplantation given in detail from 800 BC up to AD 1996. The transplant timeline details when, where and what happened from the earliest historical reports to twentieth-century scientific developments.

Author sources

In addition to the websites and books above, the author used the following materials in the writing of this book:
Website of the Department of Biological and Agricultural Engineering of North Carolina State University
Website of the United Kingdom Transplant Support Service Authority
Website of the Health System of the University of Michigan

Index